_IER GROOM

EGGPLANT

GOLDEN OR SCORNED

wrinkled sea press

Wrinkled Sea Press
P.O. Box 234
S. Orleans, Massachusetts 02662

ISBN 978-1-7377477-4-‑

Text and cover design by Charita Patamikakorn

ACKNOWLEDGMENTS

With thanks to the following people who have contributed to my journey as a poet.

Gerry Grenier, *Publisher. Thanks for this opportunity to share my poetry with a wider audience.*

David Byron, *Dear Friend, 9-29-2024.*

John Bonanni, *poet and Editor of the Cape Cod Poetry Review – a special thanks for your guidance and encouragement.*

Julie Witas, *for your suggestions during the final editing process.*

AUTHOR'S NOTE

The very act of writing this poetry has been a freeing and forgiving experience, helping me to resolve physical, mental, spiritual and emotional phases in my life.

During 2018–2019 I was struggling with severe depression and a separation from a relationship. It was during this period that my poetry began to evolve – and with encouragement from those around me I took the next logical step to share my experiences through a published book.

It is my hope that readers will be as moved reading my poetry as I am lifted by the experience of sharing.

—Albert P. Groom

AS TIME GOES ON

We allow the wounds to heal
we should not be left
with the thoughts of
which one hurts more
than another
Nor should in what order
matters
if you truly want to
let go of carrying
the pain of the past

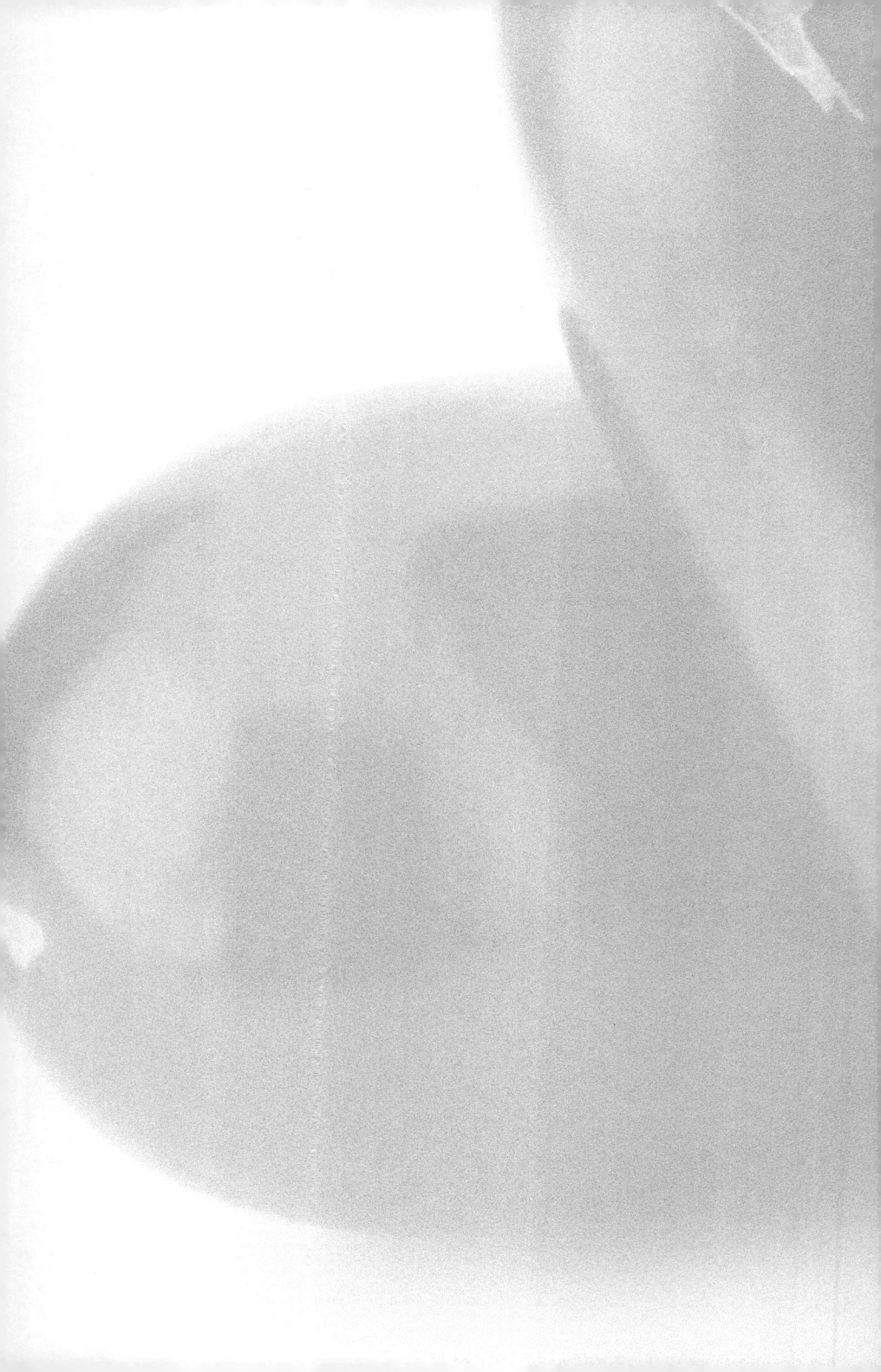

TENDER MOMENTS

As majestic as a harlequin sunrise
variegated and tender
shown with moments of precision.

So therapeutic
while my body lies still
listening to the small lap of the ocean.

Singing to me
and the other tiny creatures
waves of clouds crest the horizon.

The sands
damp and cold
under-dressed this morning.

As I hear
my daughter's teeth chattering
with chin quivering,

I hold up my wing
to comfort you, before we roll home
for hot cocoa.

To Tiana, a joy held close with my heart
Love, Poppa

POEMS

BE IN THE NOW

Freedom brings me
as far as I am willing
to let go of the problem.

When I let it fester
it has a hold on my soul
overtaking my mind
then physical mental and
spiritual damage persist.

While sitting with me
far longer
then I should ever allow.

Help bring my thoughts
out of this prison
or be dragged,

like watching a crazy dog
chew on my pant leg,
knowing I had no right
to stay there.

Detached from the fears of
yesterday and tomorrow.

Be in the now.

HOMETOWN

Entering
the maze of marsh grass

pausing to gaze
at the wispy clouds of the blue sky.

Two times taller
than I – straight in uniform,

hollow reeds
with feathered tops
dancing in the winds above.

I am lost
in the pale brown beauty,

a sanctuary
from the rest of the world.

With only one
thin skinny path,

parked in the park
of downtown Truro,

between the highway
and Old Route 6.

The only eyes on me
that of a Redwing Blackbird
sweetly singing cheerfully.

ROUNDING THIRD

For me to own my own glove
what a prized possession...

Not having much else to share
in this sport with a small class,
no time to warm the bench...

At the change of innings
often throwing the mitt
up into the air
like a graduation cap.

I aways liked the handoff;
to keep the bluestone dust out
from the moist inside,
definitely a pet peeve of mine.

Exhilarating!
rounding third
heading home
enjoying
High fives
Fist bumps.

THE CLAM

Pain and sorrow
cannot be borrowed
from anyone,
only manifested from within.

Once that lid is open
the tiniest bit, there is no telling
just where the mind might go
or how long you may stay there
on this free fall
without saying a word.

Due to the fear
of just what others may think,
you do not want to
air out your dirty laundry,
instead sitting with this
festering stink.

Though some of us would understand
and at the blink of an eye
just listen to what you might
have to share.

Instead all bottled up
for the jar does not even hiss
to allow any of this pressure
to escape from the inside.

With my head in my lap
just slouching there crying
why, why, why?

THE BEAUTIFUL SEASHELL

I once turned
into a singing bell,
before that I had to
clean out the smell.

While I sputter and stammered
saying what the hell
as it soaks in some Coke
telling you it was
far from a joke.

It did the trick while turning
brown and thick
as I stirred with a stick,
the shine after the brine
made it look quite fine
ring on.

FROM CASTLE TO CAVE

For I was not born this way.
It took the first teen years
before bottled spirit arrived,
which took me down,
hard to the ground
gut wrenched – poisoned again!!!

That hot stove burned,
searing my insides
from head to toe
within minutes – and no soft glow.

Overboard, sinking fast,
trashed on the grass
spinning round and around
spent, this unkempt gent.

Crying why?
not sure what to try
the booze in the bag
inspiring one to sag and lag
staying behind self imprisoned.

DRUGS

When I started
  again this morning
as if opening the cap
on the gunpowder barrel
leaving a trail behind.

Bound to find some
explosive reaction
for what I had done today
or days before,
since it is a constant ritual
trying to hide my addiction.

Inflicting pain to self
and most often the people
I care about most
it is an unfair trap,
snagged and pulling me
in one direction or another.

My brain is in a clamp of clouds
far from soft or puffy.

THE HAWK

As the feather floats down
from the bird chosen
to take flight and circle
the updraft
so high in our sky.

The spiritual blessing I feel
each and every time
we cross paths.

Sometimes so close
eye contact is made
that is when I can see,

the red in your pupils
and the yellow and orange
in your beak.

I've seen you fly
cutting through the trees
then stop to rest,

if I take my eyes off you
you're often lost blending
into the surroundings behind,
Thank you for your Grace.

OCTOBER SKY

As I watch the tall marsh reeds
dance, swaying in the wind
close to sunset.

I could see there feathered
shaped tops so many
spanning this estuary.

This time of year
brought on an amazing site
in preparation of another season.

In the distance a swarm
of Blackbirds drawn closer
swimming through the sky
left to right and back again.

Dropping in a twisting funnel motion,
hundreds of them following the next
it took some time to clear the air
with a few late drifters
when it was over, I just sat there in awe.

JANUARY STORM

Astronomical tides
a disturbance crossed the country
winds howled, as rains pelted down.

A steady roar, the ocean swells,
mighty waves lifting rocks
shot puts across the road.

Cliffs chewed by the strong sea,
toppled trees strewn Ballston beach
left looking like broken nest.

While nature calms
twilight escapes the horizon
the night sky begins to twinkle.

An appearance of the waxing crescent
its bright bottom shown
when full, known as the Wolf Moon.

THE MOON

The moon
 just waiting
to kiss my cheek,

all I have to do
is open the door
and look up at you.

Instead to ponder and pause
while there is nothing
stopping me
from going to see you.

Just then turning the handle
to walk out
for I don't even need
a shirt or shoes.

Here I come
always drawn to you
sometimes as a crescent sliver
or full and bright.

I could even read something
with this novel night light
choosing to make hand puppets
which will gallop and dance
across the outside wall.

SNAGGED

Rip, run or tear again
we are not talking
about pantyhose.

Instead it is like being
snagged, pulled backwards
while looking forward
for that next fix.

Whatever it may be
blinding us on how
to have the courage
to get off the messy road
with no glowing sunsets.

Drawn back even further
from family or friends,
the whole is giant
but even smaller as my
thoughts drift to my
shadowing problems.

Time stands still
as I lose track
on just where to go,
how did this happen again?

My train had no whistle
for I had No reason to get up
Somber was putting it mildly,

It was a storm
I had never faced before.
Please remember
HELP is the shortest prayer.

TIME NOT SO WELL SPENT

Had me feeling less than a gent,
I am in recovery
so now I have a different
approach
to say no to that roach.

The goal for my roll is not to
get twisted, years of that
kept me way off track
addiction only added friction.

That campaign in the
brain is so insane
I wanted to inquire just how
to inspire so I can perhaps
save you from that fire.

You're left with desire for more
telling me life is such a bore
while you sit and open
another can of Albacore
since all your
other money goes too dirt.

Unkempt unable to
sometimes
pay your rent
days could be numbered
before you're living in a tent.

I've gotten to see people
who share such stories
far from sitting in all
their glory.

BETTY

Always remembering you
after giving me a heartbeat,
black hair and brown eyes.
Things were complicated
right from the start,
as I made it home before you.

Teaching me about butterfly kisses.
My teddy bear and I felt cherished.
As you would sew Mama Bear back-up,
after I battled to hold on to her,
me – your youngest of six.

The chest was the last to fail,
repair kit once more as you
sewn on a yellow terry cloth
to her belly.

Spending many of days with you
sifting baked goods from scratch,
Lemon meringue pie
was one of my favorites.

Oh your cold hands
on my warm heart when I got sick.

Days traveled by till I cared for you a bit.
An unexpected trip to the hospital
took you away.

When I came to see you, that last day,
I asked to have the side rails lowered.

So I could jump into bed with you,
to comfort you, having to accept
this was best for you.

I still talk to you, sharing how I miss you!
Love, Albert

MAMA BEAR

It had been gray for days
steady, beyond that number
unable to count on both hands.

Spared some of the dreadful thoughts
while holding onto old Mama Bear
she turned fifty-plus a time ago.

Still wearing the dress
my mom sewed for her
over the belly that needed repair.

The remnants were from a sundress
Betty made for herself.

DELICATE

The thorny rose hip in Bloom
marks the entrance
to the path ahead.

Pink delicate petals
with a corn-yellow center,
seeing bees in their glory.

Tender and sweet as I pluck a few
Then place upon my tongue
extracting the flavor.

The wind blew rather hard
watching the salt spray
roll off the wave tops.

As a roar jetted from the surf,
loose sand swam past our feet
that sound sifting over dry seaweed.

The beachgrass was combed over
A few strays leaving swirling circles
Of magic around its foothold.

ROLLING CLOUDS

As the tear drops
   run down my face
      with head tilted.

One faster than the other
   rolling off the cheek,
      next the chin.

After hitting my thigh, over the knee
   down the shin, to my feet
      a wet salty sparkle.

Seen from a candle
      flickering above
   missing the soul of my Mama.

Knowing her spirit
   still walks with me
         in every cloud....

FLY TO DREAM

Dream to fly
the Cape Cod butterfly
one day caught my eye
with no real direction.

This dance and in all its
beauty the soft velvet wings
pale violet in color
with deeper spots.

Now stop to rest
upon its host as a guest
its appendages continue to
shutter open close in
unique motion.

For I shall remember this day
captured a forever image
only seen very few
stray away back
on the trade winds
of the amber sky.

FAREWELL

As my dog cries for me
to bring his slippers
cancer has returned
to see my friend in such pain
I did all I could do to comfort
Jessie.

I would sing, to f nd we were
doing it together
belly and eyebrow rubs
the lower back
that's always the spot.

We would take turns
resting on one another's shoulder
my furry friend
some of the best times spent.

I have been in your life
since the early days
when I could see the playful youth
in your eyes.

Today's the day cf hardship
        to have you euthanized,
the warmth of your breath
passing my neck
will always be with me.

SPARKLE

Highest in the winter sky
and long as you may
opposite summer.

I ask, have you ever seen
the crystals of snow sparkle
from your beautiful glow?

The air so dry
sound carries afar,
some nights the wind whistles
and sings, blowing through
the big old willow trees.

While watching the dry snow
swim and dance across
the buried layer of grass,
set adrift
the path to my door
fill again that night.

Between the chorus of noise
and the splendor of light
I had trouble falling asleep.

THE HANGOVER

While my head hurt
with breath awfully sour
the body feels so foul
that cry for help.

I really feel like this is it
can only dry heave and spit
the promise I can t do this anymore.

While my disease
haunts me the bedevilment
tells me I can't dc this any less.

The tug of war
where the bottle
only wins out again
sometimes Whiskey maybe Gin.

Again I smash my shin from the
choice of a flask
that path on the road I chose
is never smooth
like the burn I feel.

Crazy lazy bewildering
such emotions left not to think
about much just more self-pity,
while I spiral feel even more viral
one must learn not to roast toast
or boast
scorn and torn sure to follow
after I swallow.

Leaving you with these words
The stove is always Hot
so for me not to touch
I must leave it be
now only coffee or tea
for THEE.

SOBRIETY

For you the things that I would do
at all cost, especially
to make that call
which does not cost.

Having more than one number
is important to me
the community I seek
is special to me,
knowing someone is there
to listen while I speak.

I don't even know your last name
for I have no shame just to know
you have had a similar show
male or female at no spare
I really get to show I care.

The choice is mine
to bend my elbow for another
when that happens today
may it be while I talk
to another one of my peeps.

There to listen or maybe heard
as sometimes I wallow in my curd
this is no game, for setbacks
are real that takes one out
then forgets how to deal.

Telling ourselves no one will know
but instead back in
my head
stash, smash, crash,
bash, hash, lash and so on...

JUST DON'T TAKE IT

Make it or break it
no time to fake it
I have trouble
trying to shake it.

Loyal and royal
it's best not to spoil
and find oneself
ready to boil
left only to recoil.

That tension so hard to mention
like a lifelong pension
with an added extension.

When I say "Screw It"
it is only screwing me more
in my head
trouble to get out of bed
that pain pound oh so profound.

The sprit I seek is so bleak
a mindful image with a skull
and crossbones on its bottle
For a pill, powder or smoke
Only poison for us.

DAMN THE PUSHER MAN

The path of destruction
and in its wake
almost took the life of another.

You know who you are feeding
enough booze and drugs to others,
that yet another overdose
or even death is now
upon your dark creepy shoulders.

The haunting seems to never stop
for those harmed and their families
left to suffer through the dreadful pain,
either the first time or now addicted
or gone forever.

Upon awakening another day
thoughts and nightmares
are tapes played once again.

For the victims and loved ones
standing by, daily recovery seems
a way to cope with those days
which are now behind us.

Left to pick up the pieces
while once again you sit and wait
to prey upon another life and the life
of the souls of more families.

Seen first hand—Parent
Nov. 18th 2014

BARK

Shaded braided or even paraded
the tree twist toward the light
bold with delight
captured by the sight of many
for some would
hardly even pay a penny.

Once a mere twig I often wonder
how did you grow so big?

Your seed then roots
nestled in the crack
of a large boulder caught my sight
while looking over my shoulder.

A Conifer – hunter green needles
dark brown flaky bark large long
penile cones like the ones that
hang from the old Cuckoo clock.

To watch you sway while
the wind blows down the cavern
I found a post and beam tavern
that made me think of you today.

I only wore one shoe for the
other was trapped in your sap
I went to the outhouse looking out
the half moon crescent in the door.

Only you I could see
my tree which had me filled
with glee.
Back in the day
was carved a heart
with mine and her initials.

AS I CAST MY MAST

I was not quite so fast
the wind slowed
as the tide ebbs,

now I find myself
up on a bar
with nothing to drink
the signs are far from bright.

As the fog rolls in
and I've run aground
no light to shine
no horn to blow
as I cry out
I hear a faint hello.

I keep up my sound
as I hope to be found
next thing I knew I am
spellbound for there you are
with everything I need to be
free, I'll let you lead the way
which turns out to be a
grand old day.

FREEDOM WAS A PUFF

To ask what is my part
when I have felt
so torn apart,
wrapped up tight
coiled in fear,
being tripped up
in what my true meaning
of Freedom was.

A puff here and there
        a smokescreen
trapped in plastic
down to the corner
of the bag again.

Tiptoeing around
using only a one hitter
so my fingers don't smell
and turn brown.

The day came
of laden guilt
and shame to stub out
what I thought was
the Peace pipe.

Instead what I found,
was a wrestle – physical
mental and spiritual
with my mantra
Run Lie Hide…

AN AWAKENING

My sobriety
     is as important
as food air and water.

I did not always feel that way
for over three decades stuck
a slave to my addiction

had me thinking that was a
necessary part of my life.

The bottom line –
it was all a mind game
which left me at war with myself
and most of the time others.
Tapping into that altered state of mind
had me trapped on the negative side
in the red while in my head.

Much time spent and lost
while I flicked my Bic
uncapping my trap,
I have risen from that
prison and have learned
I don't have to go back,
today to share what I have
learned as a free spirt.

MY MOVE

Has taken me out of my groove
which in turn
I no longer feel that smooth
I choose to be stark
cause I am so in the dark
I miss my spark.

Once happy-as-a-lark
now no longer in the park
I face my space
that seems out of place &
brace for I chase my Grace.

The need to stay strong
for so long has me uptight
as if I was only wearing a
Thong.

Now it's time to break out
the Gong!

Close to the coast looks like I have
more than most
some would even boast
then start to post
not act like they wear
the shoes of a ghost...

STUCK

Your sentiment had me stuck
in the sediment,
dark and muddy
pinched by those crabs
as I sink deeper
buried up to my neck
what a suck in this muck
for I am claustrophobic
and not to use my arms
makes my breath even heavier.

As if in a hibernated state
   blood   flow   slows
       mind goes dark
as I wrestle with that word; Hope

For as I change the letters
and find I have a little   Phoe
that Phoenix lifted me up
gently placed upon the armrest
of a giant nest.

Risen from the ashes of despair
  another renewed cycle
   of growth near
    as a gentle rain came
     and slowly washed me
      of the pending gloom
       free spirit once more
        to share such a story.

RETURN

As life went dormant
the key to tranquility
was hidden from space and time.

Trouble to justify,
a sudden stalemate
was synchronized.

Clouds float past,
tides still turn,
the sun has awakened
a little bit later today.

Not seen the moon for weeks,
angles are distant,
lift me if you will, from the covers
that feel as heavy as sheets of steel.

STARS ON THE HORIZON

Oh those I get to see so far beyond
keep us happy and free
join in this grand moment
when sometimes shooting at me,
gentle and mysterious
while sparkling with glee.

The colors in the universe really
attract me, their fires so fierce
strike upon thee some mornings
a most spectacular sight
oh so heavenly.

First with a blue hue of twilight
while casting shadows
keeping us warm so bright
one could even lose their sight,
occasionally one may find
an eclipse that could scare
the panic for many is rare.

As we turn the oceans begin to churn
with a spark of hope a new day
the glow begins to grow
without this glow nothing would grow
Burn – Baked – Scorched
words used to describe our
star vibrant whatever it may.

I'm glad you're with me
upon setting while blinking
and winking to the goodbye
for another day.
Left with those memories
the emerald green light
when I close my eyes
oh so many the gifts from
the Archangel Raphael.

WAS IT BUT JUST A DREAM

As your eyes touch mine
and some time goes by
seems as though a kiss
may be bound to follow.

For I am no kid perhaps that
blends next time we meet
as the rain came down and
fear of your make up run

not a problem
as I see you wore none.

Natural as that may be
I can see your luster and gleam
which sends out a beam.

That soft gentle mist
gather on the leaves
for we have no worries

now sitting under a large maple tree
the canopy in all it's grand
keeps us dry.

Just how big?
I ask you to wrap your arms
around one side and I the other
now let's see if we can
touch our wrist or fingertips.

Just then the sun broke out
and a rainbow bound,
now what a find
that's when it happened
a kiss that felt so kind.

THE WEATHER VANE

Out in the rain wind and cold
looked up upon by many
pointing in the direction
as the strong wind blew.

Cresting another building
as I gaze I see another.
Birds stop to rest on your very top,
where I live the splendid sight
in a number of shapes and sizes

Leaves me in amaze
for I've thought of taking photos
with the sky as the backdrop,

sometimes the focal point
has been punished
hammered and damaged
by the strong Nor'easter
left askew pointing upward.

Down still the letters NEWS
below show me the direction
the weather vane I feel your pain
to stand alone and weather the storm.

With those bold letters I grouped
from above, help me to think of just
what this object is providing
in all its beauty at the peak

a fish, a whale, a mermaid,
a turtle, a sail, feathered cock
oh I meant to say rooster,
an eagle, a dog.

Maybe even a frog
may the list of expressions
go on whatever you fancy.

DELIGHTFUL

Like a deep winded dragon
with such fiery thoughts,

twinkle in the eyes,
to melt in your arms

like frosting that's being applied
to a cake yet to cool.

Smooth over the shoulder,
riding down the backbone

to the shelf of the buttocks below,
hot cross buns sticky and sweet.

Prepare for the delightful treat
until soft tender moans

render from the breath
were they official or artificial?

Only curious because at this point
it was not really important,
as the vocal vibrations were there.

WHICH WILL IT BE

Nullified   Lullabied
Purified   Butterflied

Which will it be?
Can you make it with me
and still feel as though
you have been set free?

The make up so natural
mulled on a pedestal
earth tones glisten
on your cheekbones.

It's the little things
that change thee – simple
is the way it ought to be
not in a bubble

Clear blue sky
no need to cry,
calm winds on my skin
with my puppy
rubbing against my shin.

Time to play not to stray
knowing everything will be
Okay

GROWTH

Give myself to you – blood sweat
and tears all in so few years,
I would be here if you were there
getting to show how I still care.

Now we are stretched,
branded, not banded
so rough unable to stand
the quick set foundation
helped me to view the world.

A bridge was built poured in a mold
ONLY to one day unfold,
the keystone soon fell
as rocks tumble into the waves,
that raw emotion churning away
the grandeur could not withstand
the candor of sincerity felt.

Out was the only way
I could stay dear
to help me feel clear,
anything I do seems so askew
as if I just ate a screw
brick by brick – the pages turned.

To stay in the moment
felt so helpless
only able to wallow in the stress,
thoughts soon came of
taking myself completely
out of the picture.

The spark in the distance
kept me alive
God I hope
to always remember
I am here for a reason.

SHYING AWAY

Lord my life meant
more to you than me
for I was shying away from it.

Let me not pretend
when I go to hit send
for you were the one
it was meant to go too.

In this bleak dismal pit
is where I found myself
not sure how to deal
when I woke from my trance.

I had shut down
not sure how to restart
as I hit the refresh button.

I pressed on and see me now
with a glow you
would never know
I looked like such a hoe
wanting to turn you away
today I think I will stay.

THE BALANCE IN LIFE

Ever remembering forward
is still forward

clocks do not turn backwards
only the memories we rewind.

So while there let us
not forget to take the time

to think of the kind
as to embrace the good

in all things
stand clear of the smear.

Watch the leaf, feather
or boat gently float bye

while capturing my eye rough roads
sometimes end with soft ripples

which may take longer
then one ever expects.

RISEN

Bedazzled – while the full moon
rises above the horizon,
watched from the shoreline of the beach.

As if raised from the bottom of the ocean
the feeling I get
while sharing this event with you.

Amidst the cosmic dance over the water
a shimmer trail of light creates sparkles
to be seen through the lens of your eyes.

As the waves gent e break
in this mindful meditation
spoken from the spirt of nature.

THE STRESS

Had me under arrest
in such an ache
rarely a break
the highway in my head,
upon awakening was filled
with such dread.

A constant chatter of grog
left behind
dreams and aspirations
of where I could be,
now out of focus in a blur
to ask for help from this
was so unnatural.

I was on a bend, behind the curve
where only professional help
could see me,
I found I had to stop
digging deeper
values at this point
had nothing to do with money.

Integrity Peace Connection
Gratitude Freedom
Happiness Passion Love
Amen.

CURDLED

Do you remember the day
the butterfly kissed my cheek,
back on that day I felt so weak.

My life seemed pretty bleak
for I had trouble to speak
trying to relate
to what was really going on
in my mind heart and soul.

The feeling of a giant hole
crippled thee with spite
since what I did prior took
all my might.

Lost just how to fight
life took on a new color
not so bright and that's
where I dug in tight.

Masked with such fear
Never to this extreme,
as just a short time ago
I felt so on the beam
enjoying my cream.

SONGBIRD

As I bounce
down your road
I ain't quite right
instead I ditch the fight.

It's the spoken word
since I no longer choose
to swallow my curd.

Now softly sung
from the bellows of a bird
  over and over
until I'm entranced.

Its melody so tender
had me stop to dance
I swing my hips
coming to grips
to be stern and learn
this is how I should
yearn to earn.

CATBIRD

How do I know spring
has final arrived on the Cape?
It is when the first Catbird
has been spotted.

Sharing the beautiful song
Whey whey whey
the cry of a winged cat
followed by a fluted
prolonged whistle
swhit swhit te te ta ta tha.

The head bobbing
body twitching and dancing
upon the tree limb
as time goes on
and more of you join.

Signing becomes climactic
as the morning light grows.

Your pale-gray color
whenever I see you
My heart jumps joyfully
as I sign and whistle back to you
Whey whey whey
swhit swhit te te ta ta tha.

HELD

My mind was filled
with blood clots
of what others wanted
me to do, how I should feel.

When it was me
the one having to be true
to thy own self
my records recorded
a different story,

That's how I fought off
the meat loving
Venus Flytrap
I did not fall there
a dream came along
and sucked me out of bed.

Each one of those
eyelash feelers
taunting in some way,
the bitter taste
of my salty tears
while I cry released me
from her hold
true as the day brings light.

GINGER

It took leaps and bounds
for me to come back around
like the hummingbird
so much energy expelled
in that journey
crossing the Gulf.

My short travels
had me engulfed inward
so many plates spinning and
knowing the baskets
where hard to fill.

Married we go unti they
kept saying there was no,
I in Team.

Yes, she the steamroller
flattened my patten
until I could only walk like
the Gingerbread man
with hands in the air
nothing left to carry
now deeply introverted
laying on that sheet pan
crisp, dry and baked.

SHRED HATRED

It's not what you're worth at birth,
life has its ups and downs,
stupid crowns some even hate
if you're brown; how dumbfound!!

Stop acting like such a clown,
spellbound, your bad Karma
has others hoping you may drown!

So while you are still around
and your focus of crap is always found.

May your lips be bound
so you stop that pound,
bringing so many to the ground
while all you do is hound
and make others feel unwound.

You're hoping to see a mass mound
underground, from this battle ground.

We will not sit back
without making a sound,
instead let us rebound

We will seek a turnaround
for Fairground; Shred hatred.

MORE

As my eyes grow wide
I am finding myself having
to swallow my pride
as I listen to yet another
superior statement
blanketed over the
haves and have nots.

I find this so grimace
since we all have hearts
please don't put a price tag
on mine.

I have no shame
shiny and new maybe for you,
much of the time still
in good shape to be disposed
of over and over again.

Now considered trash
as you throw around
your hot wad of cash
the price we all have to pay
while another tree be Slain.

The old pushed into a pile
where the yellow bucket roll
to crush and smash
rendered useless
for I shed another tear
to this crippling waste.

DARK TO LIGHT

Days were always cloudy
in my world this time of year,
I was troubled with fright
rippling along in one direction
or another.

The flow allowing
the beacon to grow
day or night tranquil rough
or turbulent the ride is mine
or one to be shared.

As I don't have to go it alone
like a dog happily buries a bone,
I find I must fight
since not many good things
grow in the dark.

Some days a mere spark coming
through the crack of a doorway
is all I need for my sphere
until that warm energy
falls upon me

When the parting of the Nimbus
takes place, only then
the dance of nature all around
allowing thee to be whole again.

COME BACK

Hurt people, Hurt people
words can be a dagger
to the soul.

Harsh and sudden, it happens
drained and withdrawn
music no longer holds a happy song.

Spending time
in the Valley of Darkness
with a shattered soul.

Prayers stop, the mind
tells me, I am unable
to help myself.

    The voice of a friend
     I have to visit you
       with a searchlight
         even bring a spare.

    My free, open, positive heart
    can not break your spell
    to this bedeviling hold.

Grace maybe there,
but out of sight
to my eyes.

The key to return
  is who am I helping,
    to find my way back.

To see a spark,
hope is possible
seeking the spirit of the universe,
this had me comeback
from the Depths of Despair.

MY SPIRIT GROWS

As the dewdrops dance
in the shimmering light of day
that is when I stopped to pray.

My spirit grows brighter,
muscles relax,
as the body lies still
like in Lords nature.

The air so tranquil
not a leaf to quiver.

Only when the birds
Shake things up a little
in search of life
to keep themselves
strong and growing.

As I look over to the river
three fish break the water
bodies flapping in the air
chasing bugs above,

then splash back upon entry
turning the placid
into a wave of ripples.

OCEAN SPRAY

As the vessel nestled
dry on the dock
away from its time zone
inboard outboard.

For it had no care
the only job was
to take on a sail
as I see her stand alone.

What a beauty
ribs were sleek
I am so glad I had a chance
to sneak a peek.

The sky blue hull shown
the water line
gold trim
with purple outlines.

Oh now I see a big hole
where she must've taken
quite a blow soon to be
fixed back to float.

A PASSAGE IN TIME

If you're close enough
  to see the glimmering,
    Shimmering, sparkling
        dance off the water
as waves tumble and rumble
  rendering rocks smooth.

In all its power
  there is a still a calm
    to be found
      helping one to
        become unwound
          a few of those thoughts
    that once buried deep
soon blister out.

Allowing me to weep
out here
  in the curl of nature
    as the crust peels,
      I tend to feel fine
        no longer
            in that kind of brine.

THE MAN IN THE MOON

I had been sleeping for hours
then awoken by this bright light
  shining through my window.

The moon once again visited
    from the western sky.

When this happens
    I feel comfortable,
      even warmth, the sun
bouncing off you in the night.

  I am at a greater peace
which brings a smile
    when you show up
    without a knock
or any notice for that matter.

As I go back to sleep and you
  rotate away from my vision
    I am still with you.

For all I have to do
    is close my eyes
      I can see your face.

FANTASIZING

My surge needs protection
as my coil started to unfold
rather gentle and sweet
as I jump to my feet.

Which would you have of me
a soft growl
which turns into a purr.

Just hold my hand
and you can have both,
warm and tender
while your fresh flesh
sink deep into mine.

This embrace feels so fine
as I hold on bold
never to feel cold,
heart a race
which is an unusual pace.

Now keep your mind from
wandering too far as my
clothes are still on.

SOLID

The month of June
I seem to be hot with pen
for poetry, maybe because
Gemini has cast its web.

Which I needed to shield
myself from as well as the
heat being thrown while the
glowing poker be pointed.

To protect thy self
to have an understanding
to agree to disagree
was best.

To tell myself – No
is a love word for me,
to stand my ground
not to back down and
cower like a wilted flower.

Solid I must stand
because I know I can
manage my time and
share what I believe to be kind,

I may not always be right
I am willing to be redirected
As I hope to be granted
Serenity.

DEE SIDE DID

Was there Justice to be had
or were you Just An Ass?

Close too, but foregoing trail.

The tribulations having limited
jubilations, when the dust
settled definitively.

A measured accomplishment...

As the Defendant being on guard
with my pen as my sword.

While I navigated through this
conundrum of trickery and tomfoolery
between Plaintiff
and her lawyer.

Touche' was the torch
I had to bare
as the metal strike
and another coin drop.

The school of hard knocks
has a room
without any clocks.

STORMY

The words you spoke
torpedoed through my heart
as if shot from a cannon
at close range.

This event
may still sit deep within
only when calm
can I hear the gentle
sounds of a Chickadee
singing to me.

I no longer hear
those Boisterous lungs
that once charged my way,
Instead I let the sound
of wind blowing the leaves
to ruffle my feathers.

REPOSITION

The light coming through
the keyhole
of the darkest day,

tear drops drip
having a carving force
as grand as the greatest canyon.

Thoughts uneven,
while they roll down my sides
into a pond of the past.

Ripples fierce
with no mirror image,
far from placid.

Eyes swell, vision blurred
my tears left watermarks
on the pages,

the felt marker run
so I thought I was done
but now even more obscure.

FORGIVENESS

How free do you want to be?
a ransacked heart
has trouble sharing a pulse.

Stop letting hope
grope your soul
with its unforgiving toll.

In the light of prayer,
come back and share,
the tunnel need not funnel
you in despair any longer.

The path that carries me today
should not be the one
I was dwelling upon yesterday.

FORGED

To really appreciate
the twisted metal
on the old iron gate.

Forged from the fire
pounding the large anvil.

Cloaked in leather
to protect thee,
water near
to cool the sizzle.

The ornate flares
come to life, one strike
after another, mapped
from the gifted creator.

Twirled feathers swirl
over the heavy canvas,
breath taking
captured by the artist.

THE WAR

While in my room I could see
        the candle flicker
though the walls were thick
and the sounds muffled
I could still hear the two of you.

It was the tone
which crept into my bones,
using my blanket as comfort
pulling on the threads.

As I squeeze my pillow
        oh so tight
starting to rock myself
until my bed creeks.

Not fond of the sound
when I can hear my clock tick
but that's where I allowed
my mind to go.

Soon after my candle
burned out on its own
the fuel was gone
and so was mine
I briefly felt safe tonight.

PRISM OF DARKNESS

The explosions rocking this world
growing even more painful, children
hoping they may still hold mother's hand.

Home now in shards
  "Where does one go?"
        Father sent to fight.

Perhaps never to be seen again
    an unwelcome farewell
          ears ringing.

Birds
  no longer singing
      the music I once knew.

The water dripping
   into the washbasin
        when mother washed my face.

Eyes cry, with even more fear
   upon my shoulders,
        while you shell my soul
            unable too shed another tear.

THE BUZZ

I once lived in time
where it was common
to see a bush in bloom
and the sound of the buzz
its frequency giving me
goosebumps.

Wings flapping so fast
some so heavy with pollen
at times would make takeoff
tricky.

Nesting in a nearby steeple
they stop at the
birdbath
to strengthen their cast.

Even though they can sting
and swarm
today I ask where have you
all gone...

These days encased
I'll make you a hive
where I'll help you survive
lost but not forgotten
We need you.

WISHING

Wishing doesn't work in recovery
it's not a program of magic
and if wishes cured addiction
we would have been well long ago.

Growth is not the result
of wishing
but of action and prayer
have a great day
and enjoy the joy of being
sober today!!!

It's not where we were that
counts but where we are going,

pack your bags
and move out of your past
into a present filled with hope,
keep moving forward
and enjoy the gift today.

SKIPPED A BEAT

The heart is made up of thread
cords of string, blood and tissue.

Sometimes it feels as though
a bug has landed
on mine,
tugging and pulling trying to
get away as I really wish
you would stay, dear to mine.

So I ask why
would you have to stray
and venture away
while I feel maybe
you have quickly fled.

A tune that leaves me
with even more questions
now challenged in wonder
are you the one that got away.

Instead let me go back to that day
and remember the good and uncomfortable
for a new friend
could have abound
I guess not this round.

BOUNDARIES

Friends come and go
some think
there ought to be
more than that
weighing in
principals
over personalities.

Pushing, twisting,
demanding truths
until emotional behavior
becomes sharp and harsh
as one side frames
name calling.

Feeding
their tweaked concept,
words are powerful
although saying nothing
not reacting
has the strength
of the greater good.

If you're Cross with me
it's not mine to Bear
Now off of my Cloud.

HOOT

The moon I see
as we share
in the prism of darkness,

such a welcomed guest,
the phase to be in now
with its brightest glow.

With this light I was able
to open my book tonight
and read to you
a gesture of some poetry.

For this one
I spun with some silly romance
so now seem to be the right time
to read this flow,

with the crickets as my chorus
suddenly the hoot of an owl
had me pause.

For I wanted us to hear
what nature had to spare
before I went on
I can always do this over
not in fear of getting it right.

THE SANDBOX

So grand with every grain of sand
sharp dull or smooth
often is found in my shoes
with each step
the boundless beauty.

I also get to see
and hear the souncs
of the abundant liquid.

Rolling, crashing, soraying
some mornings still tranquil
placid like
the image of a mirror
reflecting the sky back to me.

I am relieved of self-pity
finding myself,
mind washed clear
of any hammer.

I may gaze at a shell
entranced by its spell I don't
have to be challenged
just absorb the warn rays.

Some days
my footsteps are the only
ones I can see as I know
I am carried here

to see the endless creativity,
bound to bring some home
as I play ever ingrained
in good memories.

TOUCHED

I am as spiritual as a rose
that still bleeds
after you have gone,
departing from this land
to a better place.

From red to golden
like on the most beautiful
sunset ever seen
dancing off the colors
of your hair.

Shadowing a violet silhouette
as you drift towards the horizon
being lowered
feeling as though, taken away
spirit has gifted you over time
as you have touched many.

TEARS

Some tears drop more
persistently than others,
I cannot tell you why
perhaps some love
digs deeper
into our hearts than others.

It's a real bummer
when my thoughts join
and you are no longer with me
loss was sudden, then amplified.

For I could no longer
look into your velvet eyes
you were gone but not lost
as the memories hold true
in the time our paths cross
may the plank of sorrow
be slightly softer tomorrow.

IN THE MOMENT

As the sea fog dances above
the water somewhat eerie
at first light, my what a sight

I stopped to gaze
at a couple of swans
their beauty and grace
had me so fond
in this moment.

Now I sit and ponder
memories pass
across my mind
some I strain to find
while I stop and unwind
after a week of the grind.

It's the small stuff that
sets me free
to smell a rose
rather than just walk by,
that is being in the now.

VIBRANT

As time goes by
I fall prey to the love in your eyes
the crevice in your dimples
are the deepest.

Your silhouette – while wearing
a long flowing dress
covers you so well.

Stunning – green
against your auburn hair
flowing over the shoulder
blends into your instrument.

As we stand so close
your violin past my skin
before you brought it to your chin.

The mind takes root
when you gently ride the reed
over the strings.

Listening with my eyes closed
vibrant vibrations felt within
melting into the music.

IRRELEVANT

Happiness is a byproduct!

The empty nest is where
I fare to rest,

It's all good or not
a choice
which I allow to be mine.

When loneliness shows
for this is a place I can go
as my bed in my head
is not big enough for you.

Well let me go to you
analyze to take action
with a question
how much
is fact or just fiction?

If it's a game have no
time too tame any blame.

Don't feed on what
is not important...

AS I FIND MY 7 AM ALARM

Clock to have no
snooze button
a row of Mack's
start their engines.

Upon their turn
thick gray smoke bellows
from their stacks
the air far from fresh.

Then the big cat starts
and proceeds to load boulders
into the trucks
with a bulldog on her hood.

The enormous
thundering rattle of metal
dropped upon the steel
        EARTHQUAKE!

Now ready
the equipment moves
BEEP BEEP BEEP
buckets of dry sand to follow
which turns into a dust storm
growing in its plume again
another morning.

ADRIFT

Reading from Shakespeare
to the head of a spear
was never at a loss
since my cross
does not weigh me down.

Lifted as I drifted
my ship had already sailed
far from plain as she wore
the colors of a rainbow.

Not carrying any cannon balls
only ropes and swings of love
made of the finest silk
from the spiders on board.

As we weave our way
around the chain of islands
selling whatever art spun
in days before
beauty and blessings captured
woven from the heart.

FREE

The invasion of morning light
is natural, today
as we spin in the universe.

Our blue planet,
floating in a dance,
rotating, successfully another day.

What colors the sky may bare
determined by where you stand
at any given moment.

Clouds like feathers, wisp along
a bulk of pillows, perhaps
one could float upon.

Majestic at times
as rays of light cast beams
to the heavens.

Over the tranquil waters
captures a mirror image
let's me be free...

SPADE

The world shown better before the light was turned on
and the color of skin now visible.

Fear set into every eye,
bones felt broken and tattered,
even though it was just thoughts in the mind.

The past had cropped up, frightens again,
damn wished the shovel was put down long ago.

Flat or spade the pain is as real as,
the feelings that run through the hollow.

Mama cried while giving birth,
just like the English Miss.
the bonnet a worldly difference,
to tell the outcome of where one is from.

Simply being born should not be a crime,
already fenced in, unable to boarder those beasts out.

Your Confederate flag fly over, sharing the same sun
and fresh air still never enough to this day.

To watch the sunset until flattening upon the horizon,
soon knowing another darkness near.

On the trail again with miles to go,
the key to freedom not always measured in how
    far the journey.

AN ANIMAL WITH NO HEART

Even birds cry, why? Ruthless terror fills the land
The line in the sands are now tines in our birth marks
An upheaval covers all the grandeur

A pact to wager war against the innocent band
With no signs, which way should we run question mark?
Even birds cry, why? Ruthless terror fills the land

A broken token of love, missing the rich
    coniferous woodland
Pressed unable to rest, like an unwelcome oligarch
An upheaval covers all the grandeur

The priceless cost of bloodshed over our
    unarmed farmlands
It's simply Unorthodox, deliberately casting a cruel Paradox
Even birds cry, why? Ruthless terror fills the land

Insane pain, inflicting so much damage to the motherland
Holding my baby, rocking back and forth in the park
An upheaval covers all the grandeur

The defective wrath on this country is affecting the
    world's command
With a target on your back nobody is willing to light
    the trigger spark
Even birds cry, why? Ruthless terror fills the land
An upheaval of evil covers all the grandeur

THE RAINBOW

Shooting pleasure
from my roots
what an array
which never goes away
up to the crown
carry me astray
over the bay
let's stop and pray
off in the distance
a burst of light
for I see a rainbow
and it strikes thee
what a span
as far as the eye could see
over the water
and onto the land
all the colors ever so grand
it was there and now she's gone
her prism-filled pleasure
what a purpose
struck by the beam
that was cast
will be a memory forever

DROPLETS

As the copper rain
rides over the shade
of the patina umbrella,

these droplets of jewels
have a profound sparkle,
with the sheen of gold.

Felt in its dance,
transpires a fall of life,
speaking a fluent sound.

The thick translucent trickle
to a bed of river rocks
that shelters the base below.

RED

Finding love with the sunset
as she crested
beneath the horizon.

A universal transformation
for another day,
playing with all thoughts stored,

feeling your heat
since I wear a burn
upon my skin.

Lobster red
from head to the shin
forgot to cover up,

now blisters bubble
hung over
de – high – dread.

In bed – chill'n out
as the thin cotton sheets
feel like sand paper.

TRAPPED

Everyday picking that wound – making you weep and cry –
never able to feel sky high – the clasp of the past –
has tunneled into the soul –
as the rivets pop within –
gives you nowhere to run –
those same thoughts –
as if chasing a bullet –
that rattles the skull –
the finger tips, now incredibly dull –
the spell, that has you reeled –
into a shallow hell –
Dark- no shadows to cast –
no flames to see –
no warmth to feel –
trapped and riddled with ill will –
dry, chapped and cracked –
the brain so insane –
stuffed with such pain –
Conflict – still self inflicted – till a spark is found –
how is one able to come back around & someday rebound

EMPIRE

Shadows long,
 trees gone
  the sky has been
   scraped.

                    Streets crossed,
                     red, yellow and green
                      blinking at every block.

So loud,
 very hard to hear
  you softly talk.

                    Man holes,
                     dodging land mines
                      fresh and often days old

Checkered bees
 on wheels,
  a screeching chorus
   as they brake.

                    Jack hammer,
                     hustle and bustle
                      my mind turns out
                       the sorest muscle

DENTIST ON 80 GOLF TERMS

The semi rough, lumberjack, golfer,
with big dog, dimples, has sweet spot,
divots, in the teeth, upper right foursomes,
#'s 11,12,13,14 hole in one, thin break.

Doctor with strong grip, choked down,
a half shot, pick up, flat stick, tester,
press, push, spotted, freshie cavity,
back, halve a hole, major, chili dip, grove.

Knock down, set up, drained, bad, whiff,
carry, angle of attack, shank, wedge,
slice, tap, hook, uncock, reload,
tee off, mudder, plugged, double bogey.

Center shaft, alignment, embedded, buried,
yank, pull, take away, gimme relief,
free drop, even short sided, impact position,
nip it, follow – through, release, recovery.

Snake, hustler, "A" Game, green, bandit,
zinger, goofed-it, flub, flop, hacker, tight
juicy lie, frogged, penalty, come back,
bump and run, burn, gross score.

THE RANT

Book me a brook; I shall
have it defended bv a Rook,
in the stream is where I wish
to let out my screams.

Verbs of profanity
are a bountiful ream
as I scowl in such foul.

I once had it recorded
then I played it back
wanting to know just who
the hell it was?

As I listened some-more,
now in fear is someone
out to get me?
Maybe a wild boar?

Sounds of the Italian mafia
came through the recorder
as I play back once more
in this share, Holy crap the
good Lord somehow taped
me on this rant.

A tremble of what was said
I had trouble to recant
at a push of a button
it was erased from

the tape, but in that moment
ever ingrained in my mind.

RELEASED

The sun shown through
the Mackerel sky
giving us this crackled
look and feel
scarlet and crimson colors
seen that morning
on the underbelly
of this blanket
breathtaking the horizon
my, those features of
nature so grand
somewhat eerie
no wind blowing
time laps
puts me in a trance
while my coffee brews
forget about you
exploring the endless joy
this framed by the Lord
blessed upon me
we can drop the rock
even if its only
a pebble in the shoe
no need to carry that
pain no matter how small

OUTER CAPE FAMILY HISTORY

As told by my mother, Betty Gray Groom, the family's historian

Mother's great Grandfather Antonio Silverio Correiro and Great Grandmother Maria De Souza were married in the village church of Capelo, Faial, Azores Islands. Children from this marriage were Nancy, Flora, Mary, Frank Antonio, Thomas William, Joseph Silverio and Elizabeth's Grandfather John De Souza. Siblings Thomas, Nancy and Flora Correiro settled in Brazil. Thomas owned a coffee plantation, married and had one son. Nancy and Flora married late in life and had no children.

Her Grandfather John De Souza Correiro was born in the village of Capelo, Faial, Azores Islands on February 17, 1847. At fourteen, he shipped before the mast on a whaling ship; this trip took him to the Indian Ocean and ports of Africa. Returning to the Azores, he traveled aboard another ship for the Islands of Madagascar through the Mozambique channel and other ports of Africa. By the time he returned to the Azores at twenty one, he had sailed the seven seas. He later came to America in 1868. He shipped aboard an American fishing boat and fished off the Grand Banks. While the ship docked in a Boston Port for repairs, John visited his brothers Joseph and Frank Correiro of North Truro, Mass. and his sister Mary, who had married Francis Peters of North Truro. John came back to North Truro in 1870 and, in 1871 Joseph, Frank, and John Correiro took the name of Gray legally when they were naturalized, being told that Correiro was the American name for Gray.

* * * * *

On November 29, 1871 John (now Gray) and Filomena Perry from Dighton, Mass. were married in the Congregational Church in Truro, Mass. Children of this marriage were Mary Gray, Joseph William Gray, John Gray Jr., Frank Perry Gray, Antone Silva Gray.

Filomena Gray died in 1885. John Gray was told of her death by a passing Provincetown fishing boat while fishing off the Grand Banks. In 1887 John Gray remarried Caroline A. Lial.

Caroline's Grandparents, Catherine Anna Francis (born Catrina Anika Francisco) and John (Joas) Chavelle were married in the village church of Santa Maria, Pico, Azores Islands on May 10, 1817. They had one daughter, Maria DeGloria Chavelle born July 18,1818. Joseph Silverio Lial and Maria DeGloria Chavelle were married April 25, 1839 in Pico, Azores Islands. Children from this marriage were Adelaide Maria, John C. Anna DeGloria, Rita DeGloria, and Caroline Augusta. Caroline was born in the village of Santa Maria, Pico, Azores Islands on February 27, 1867.

* * * * *

"By trade" Caroline had served as a dressmaker's helper for five cents a day. She came to America in 1886 and landed in Provincetown June 8, 1886, bringing with her a neighbor's niece who was coming to Provincetown to live with her Uncle Manual Rogers; "Hands Up'" was his nickname. He agreed to stand Caroline Lial's Bonds for caring for his niece on the voyage and would be responsible for Caroline for one year until she found work or married. She found work in a Shirt Factory and boarded with Mr. & Mrs. Manual Enos, known as the "Kitty Family" who took in boarders who had no relatives to come to. She stayed there until she married John Gray of Truro, a widower with five children.

John Gray and Caroline A. Lial were married at St. Peter's Church Provincetown Mass. January 8, 1887. Children from this marriage were Clara Gray, Filomena Gray, Nancy Gray, Nellie Maybelle Gray, Eva Marion Gray, Catherine Anna Gray, *Ernest Maxwell Gray, *William Joseph Gray, Leonard Allen Gray, Manuel Francis Gray and my Grandfather Thomas William Gray.

Three of John's sons were servicemen from Truro in WWI: Antone Silva Gray, Ernest Maxwell Gray and William Joseph Gray, for whom William Gray Square in Truro Center is named.

* * * * *

My Grandfather Thomas William Gray was born in Truro, Mass. on July 2, 1890. Thomas Gray married Mary Elizabeth Frazier on April 17, 1912 at Lady Of Lourdes Church in Wellfleet, Mass. Children from this marriage were Robert W. Gray, Rita E. Gray, Marjorie E. Gray, Ernestine M. Gray, Thomas W. Jr. Gray, Elizabeth M. Gray.

Thomas Gray, a builder, bought property on Old Route 6 in Truro, where he built a house in 1932. The foundation was poured by hand. His daughter Elizabeth Marie Gray (Betty) – my mother – was born there on September 10, 1932.

* * * * *

Family homestead as built in 1932

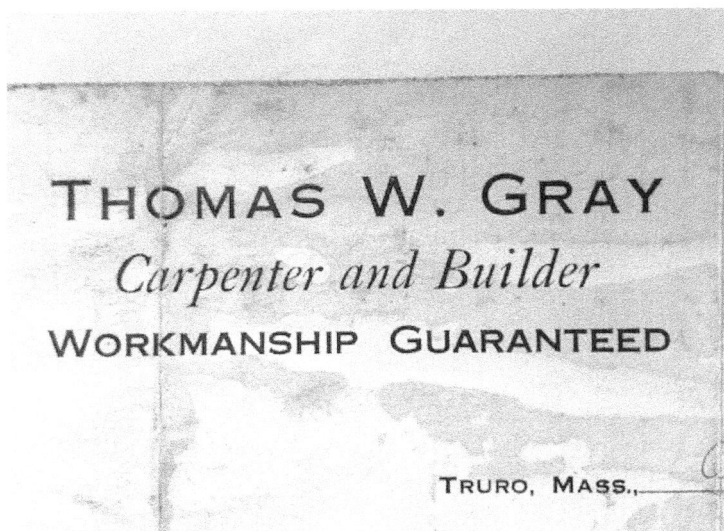

THOMAS W. GRAY
Carpenter and Builder
WORKMANSHIP GUARANTEED

TRURO, MASS.,

Grandfather's letterhead used for his business

Thomas W. Gray died October 17, 1948 and his body was waked in the house he built.

Grandmother Mary E. Gray was referred to by Mom as Nana. She worked as a chambermaid at the North Truro Highland House, now a historic hotel building, serving as the Highland House Museum. She also worked for The Western Union Telegraph Co. as a Telegraph Agent.

As Nana grew older she would sing, "The Old Gray Mare Ain't What She Used To Be." Grampy owned a 1/4 acre lot at the edge of North Pamet Road and the Pamet River. This is where the family had a garden plot. This parcel of property was taken by the state for short money in preparation of the Grand Army of the Republic Highway. Mom shared how the Army Corp of Engineers brought Route 6 through Truro in 1954 crossing the Pamet River. Sounding the river for quicksand was conducted to determine how far to pile drive the steel bars for the pilings of the bridge overpass. Bulldozers pulled the soil from the Northern hillside to the river bank for backfill. Mom shared "the house shook for days." Grandmother Mary Gray housed the engineers that sounded the river.

* * * * *

Mom, known as Betty to many, shared a vast array of memories. She referred to her father as Grampy. He was a carpenter and caretaker; one of the homes he visited was the property of the Edward Hopper House overlooking Cape Cod Bay.

Mom shared that when she was eight years old, she watched the glow from the Methodist South Truro Meeting House burning in the southern night sky in 1940; it burned to the ground. Later the family spent time collecting glass, old nails and melted pieces of brass from the old bell.

She spoke of the fowl moment of a beheading at the old wooden stump Grampy would use as a chopping block. To truly watch a chicken run around with its head cut off.

Betty spent her teenage years working on the McMillan's Pier in Provincetown shucking scallops.

* * * * *

Grandparents' 25th Wedding Anniversary

Mom Betty on Provincetown Pier at McMillan Wharf

Betty returned to the homestead in Truro with her husband Richard Joseph Groom and their six children in 1966, shortly after I was born (Albert Peter Groom). My older siblings are Christine Marie Gray, Warren W. Gray, Herbert Joseph Groom, Elmer Thomas Groom and Thomas Sean Groom.

A majority of the time Mom spent tending to the house while raising the family. She was an avid knitter of sweaters, afghans, hats and mittens and also spent her time baking Portuguese sweetbread and preserving hand picked fruits – boiling jars and melting wax during the process.

On laundry days, the boys' personal garments would hang on the clothesline with their first initials written onto the clothing tags, spelling out W H E A T. In the mid 1980's she worked at Aronld's Bike Rental on Commercial Street, Provincetown.

Betty's rich knowledge of the Outer Cape and Truro in particular was recorded in hundreds of scrap books which were later gifted to the Town of Truro.

www.ingramcontent.com/pod-product-compliance
Ingram Content Group UK Ltd.
Pitfield, Milton Keynes, MK11 3LW, UK
UKHW040615141224
452011UK00001B/11

9 781737 747741